Francis Frith's
# AROUND WINCHESTER

PHOTOGRAPHIC MEMORIES

# Francis Frith's
# AROUND WINCHESTER

◆

John Bainbridge

THE FRANCIS FRITH COLLECTION

FRITH
BOOK Co

First published in the United Kingdom in 2000 by
Frith Book Company Ltd

British Library Cataloguing in Publication Data

Around Winchester
John Bainbridge
ISBN 1-85937-139-6

Frith Book Company Ltd
Frith's Barn, Teffont,
Salisbury, Wiltshire SP3 5QP
Tel: +44 (0) 1722 716 376
Email: info@frithbook.co.uk
www.frithbook.co.uk


Printed and bound in Great Britain

*Front Cover:* **Winchester, High Street 1928**  80887

# CONTENTS

# FRANCIS FRITH: *Victorian Pioneer*

FRANCIS FRITH, Victorian founder of the world-famous photographic archive, was a complex and multitudinous man. A devout Quaker and a highly successful Victorian businessman, he was both philosophic by nature and pioneering in outlook.

By 1855 Francis Frith had already established a wholesale grocery business in Liverpool, and sold it for the astonishing sum of £200,000, which is the equivalent today of over £15,000,000. Now a multi-millionaire, he was able to indulge his passion for travel. As a child he had pored over travel books written by early explorers, and his fancy and imagination had been stirred by family holidays to the sublime mountain regions of Wales and Scotland. 'What a land of spirit-stirring and enriching scenes and places!' he had written. He was to return to these scenes of grandeur in later years to 'recapture the thousands of vivid and tender memories', but with a different purpose. Now in his thirties, and captivated by the new science of photography, Frith set out on a series of pioneering journeys to the Nile regions that occupied him from 1856 until 1860.

## INTRIGUE AND ADVENTURE

He took with him on his travels a specially-designed wicker carriage that acted as both dark-room and sleeping chamber. These far-flung journeys were packed with intrigue and adventure. In his life story, written when he was sixty-three, Frith tells of being held captive by bandits, and of fighting 'an awful midnight battle to the very point of surrender with a deadly pack of hungry, wild dogs'. Sporting flowing Arab costume, Frith arrived at Akaba by camel seventy years before Lawrence, where he encountered 'desert princes and rival sheikhs, blazing with jewel-hilted swords'.

During these extraordinary adventures he was assiduously exploring the desert regions bordering the Nile and patiently recording the antiquities and peoples with his camera. He was the first photographer to venture beyond the sixth cataract. Africa was still the mysterious 'Dark Continent', and Stanley and Livingstone's historic meeting was a decade into the future. The conditions for picture taking confound belief. He laboured for hours in his wicker dark-room in the sweltering heat of the desert, while the volatile chemicals fizzed dangerously in their trays. Often he was forced to work in remote tombs and caves where conditions were cooler. Back in London he exhibited his photographs and was 'rapturously cheered' by members of the Royal Society. His reputation as a photographer was made overnight. An eminent modern historian has likened their impact on the population of the time to that on our own generation of the first photographs taken on the surface of the moon.

## VENTURE OF A LIFE-TIME

Characteristically, Frith quickly spotted the opportunity to create a new business as a specialist publisher of photographs. He lived in an era of immense and sometimes violent change. For the poor in the early part of Victoria's reign work was a drudge and the hours long, and people had precious little free time to enjoy themselves.

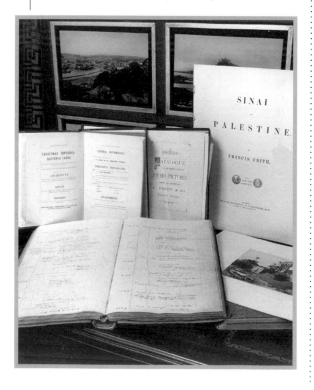

Most had no transport other than a cart or gig at their disposal, and had not travelled far beyond the boundaries of their own town or village. However, by the 1870s, the railways had threaded their way across the country, and Bank Holidays and half-day Saturdays had been made obligatory by Act of Parliament. All of a sudden the ordinary working man and his family were able to enjoy days out and see a little more of the world.

With characteristic business acumen, Francis Frith foresaw that these new tourists would enjoy having souvenirs to commemorate their days out. In 1860 he married Mary Ann Rosling and set out with the intention of photographing every city, town and village in Britain. For the next thirty years he travelled the country by train and by pony and trap, producing fine photographs of seaside resorts and beauty spots that were keenly bought by millions of Victorians. These prints were painstakingly pasted into family albums and pored over during the dark nights of winter, rekindling precious memories of summer excursions.

## THE RISE OF FRITH & CO

Frith's studio was soon supplying retail shops all over the country. To meet the demand he gathered about him a small team of photographers, and published the work of independent artist-photographers of the calibre of Roger Fenton and Francis Bedford. In order to gain some understanding of the scale of Frith's business one only has to look at the catalogue issued by Frith & Co in 1886: it runs to some 670

court card, but there was little room for illustration. In 1899, a year after Frith's death, a new card measuring 5.5 x 3.5 inches became the standard format, but it was not until 1902 that the divided back came into being, with address and message on one face and a full-size illustration on the other. *Frith & Co* were in the vanguard of postcard development, and Frith's sons Eustace and Cyril continued their father's monumental task, expanding the number of views offered to the public and recording more and more places in Britain, as the coasts and countryside were opened up to mass travel.

Francis Frith died in 1898 at his villa in Cannes, his great project still growing. The archive he created continued in business for another seventy years. By 1970 it contained over a third of a million pictures of 7,000 cities, towns and villages. The massive photographic record Frith has left to us stands as a living monument to a special and very remarkable man.

pages, listing not only many thousands of views of the British Isles but also many photographs of most European countries, and China, Japan, the USA and Canada – note the sample page shown above from the hand-written *Frith & Co* ledgers detailing pictures taken. By 1890 Frith had created the greatest specialist photographic publishing company in the world, with over 2,000 outlets – more than the combined number that Boots and WH Smith have today! The picture on the right shows the *Frith & Co* display board at Ingleton in the Yorkshire Dales. Beautifully constructed with mahogany frame and gilt inserts, it could display up to a dozen local scenes.

## POSTCARD BONANZA

◆

The ever-popular holiday postcard we know today took many years to develop. In 1870 the Post Office issued the first plain cards, with a pre-printed stamp on one face. In 1894 they allowed other publishers' cards to be sent through the mail with an attached adhesive halfpenny stamp. Demand grew rapidly, and in 1895 a new size of postcard was permitted called the

# Frith's Archive: *A Unique Legacy*

FRANCIS FRITH'S legacy to us today is of immense significance and value, for the magnificent archive of evocative photographs he created provides a unique record of change in 7,000 cities, towns and villages throughout Britain over a century and more. Frith and his fellow studio photographers revisited locations many times down the years to update their views, compiling for us an enthralling and colourful pageant of British life and character.

We tend to think of Frith's sepia views of Britain as nostalgic, for most of us use them to conjure up memories of places in our own lives with which we have family associations. It often makes us forget that to Francis Frith they were records of daily life as it was actually being lived in the cities, towns and villages of his day. The Victorian age was one of great and often bewildering change for ordinary people, and though the pictures evoke an impression of slower times, life was as busy and hectic as it is today.

We are fortunate that Frith was a photographer of the people, dedicated to recording the minutiae of everyday life. For it is this sheer wealth of visual data, the painstaking chronicle of changes in dress, transport, street layouts, buildings, housing, engineering and landscape that captivates us so much today. His remarkable images offer us a powerful link with the past and with the lives of our ancestors.

## TODAY'S TECHNOLOGY

Computers have now made it possible for Frith's many thousands of images to be accessed almost instantly. In the Frith archive today, each photograph is carefully 'digitised' then stored on a CD Rom. Frith archivists can locate a single photograph amongst thousands within seconds. Views can be catalogued and sorted under a variety of categories of place and content to the immediate benefit of researchers. Inexpensive reference prints can be created for them at the touch of a mouse button, and a wide range of books and other printed materials assembled and published for a wider, more general readership - in the next twelve months over a hundred Frith local history titles will be published! The

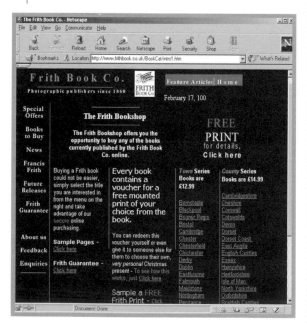

See Frith at www. frithbook.co.uk

day-to-day workings of the archive are very different from how they were in Francis Frith's time: imagine the herculean task of sorting through eleven tons of glass negatives as Frith had to do to locate a particular sequence of pictures! Yet the archive still prides itself on maintaining the same high standards of excellence laid down by Francis Frith, including the painstaking cataloguing and indexing of every view.

It is curious to reflect on how the internet now allows researchers in America and elsewhere greater instant access to the archive than Frith himself ever enjoyed. Many thousands of individual views can be called up on screen within seconds on one of the Frith internet sites, enabling people living continents away to revisit the streets of their ancestral home town, or view places in Britain where they have enjoyed holidays. Many overseas researchers welcome the chance to view special theme selections, such as transport, sports, costume and ancient monuments.

We are certain that Francis Frith would have heartily approved of these modern developments, for he himself was always working at the very limits of Victorian photographic technology.

## THE VALUE OF THE ARCHIVE TODAY

Because of the benefits brought by the computer, Frith's images are increasingly studied by social historians, by researchers into genealogy and ancestory, by architects, town planners, and by teachers and schoolchildren involved in local history projects. In addition, the archive offers every one of us a unique opportunity to examine the places where we and our families have lived and worked down the years. Immensely successful in Frith's own era, the archive is now, a century and more on, entering a new phase of popularity.

## THE PAST IN TUNE WITH THE FUTURE

Historians consider the Francis Frith Collection to be of prime national importance. It is the only archive of its kind remaining in private ownership and has been valued at a million pounds. However, this figure is now rapidly increasing as digital technology enables more and more people around the world to enjoy its benefits.

Francis Frith's archive is now housed in an historic timber barn in the beautiful village of Teffont in Wiltshire. Its founder would not recognize the archive office as it is today. In place of the many thousands of dusty boxes containing glass plate negatives and an all-pervading odour of photographic chemicals, there are now ranks of computer screens. He would be amazed to watch his images travelling round the world at unimaginable speeds through network and internet lines.

The archive's future is both bright and exciting. Francis Frith, with his unshakeable belief in making photographs available to the greatest number of people, would undoubtedly approve of what is being done today with his lifetime's work. His photographs, depicting our shared past, are now bringing pleasure and enlightenment to millions around the world a century and more after his death.

# AROUND WINCHESTER

## *The City of Kings and Priests*

WINCHESTER. THE CAPITAL city of Wessex and a history lesson in every stone of its streets. For this old place began to play an important role in the nation's past from the time the Romans founded their market town of Venta Belgarum on the site of enclosures left there by the conquered Iron Age tribe, the Belgae, on the banks of the River Itchen.

Though no one knows for certain where the bones of Alfred the Great actually rest, this was the heart of his Wessex; the capital of his old age and a refuge of peace and learning after long years of struggle fending off the Danes. Interestingly, the Anglo-Saxon Chronicle lists very few visits by Alfred to Winchester - perhaps his sojourns there were just taken for granted. His son Edward the Elder, if anything, really deserves the connection and some kind of statue, for it was he who founded the important New Minster that was to be his father's burial place.

Generations earlier in the year 643 a Minster church had been established in the town by Alfred's Saxon forbear Cenwalh. Thirty years later Bishop Haeddi arrived in Winchester and made that building his Cathedral. Alfred the Great was originally buried in the Old Minster of Cenwalh's foundation before his bones were transferred to the New Minster. In the century after his death, Winchester became the most important religious centre in northern Europe.

The Norman Conquest saw the removal of the Saxon Bishop Stigand, his Norman replacement Walkelin beginning the construction of the huge Cathedral we see today on a site roughly adjacent to the Old Minster. The nave, supposedly the longest in Europe, stretches away from the visitor entering at the western end "a vista of magnificence which, almost like the first sight of the sea or the Alps, impresses itself upon the memory for one's life".

A walk along the north aisle brings the visitor to the tomb of Jane Austen. To one side is a commemorative window to this fine novelist and a plaque to remind us of her role in English Letters - something her black marble tombstone fails to do. Nor is she the only writer buried within. Izaak Walton, author of The Compleat Angler, that wonderful tribute to contemplation and the English countryside, rests not far away in the Chapel of St John the Evangelist.

"Nowhere in England do the stones speak more eloquently of past times than in Winchester, the city of kings and priests", wrote two Victorian residents. And a fair number of both kings and priests lie with the precincts of the Cathedral; bishops such as William of Edington, and William of Wykeham, the founder of Winchester College and instigator of the reconstructed nave in the 14th century. Swithun, whose elevation to sainthood made Winchester a destination for medieval pilgrims was also originally buried here. Only one miracle is ascribed to Swithun during his lifetime - the restoration of a basket of eggs dropped and smashed by a local woman. But the pilgrims came because of the miracles and cures that are supposed to have happened after the burial of the former bishop.

On the presbytery screens are four mortuary chests (two more are reproductions) containing the bones of Swithun, several ancient Saxon kings, a handful of early bishops and those of King Canute and the unfortunate King William Rufus. During restoration work in the reign of Henry VIII, the bones were reinterred within these caskets, because there was no way of knowing who was who. As the old chronicler says: "Not knowing which were kings and which were bishops, because there were no inscriptions over the monuments...Henry placed in leaden sarcophagi kings and bishops, bishops and kings all mixed together".

There are many other delights within the building, from exquisite wall paintings dating back to the Crusades, to the famous Winchester Bible which dates from the 12th century and is perhaps the finest illustrated book in England. Elsewhere, a flight of steps leads down to the crypt. Given the marshy nature of the ground on which the cathedral stands this often floods after the rains of winter. It is now adorned with a modern statue of a human figure, called Sound II, which often stands in the water.

As we can see from the photographs, the tower is modest in size compared to the towers of many other British cathedrals. In 1107 Bishop Walkelin's original tower collapsed on to the tomb of King William Rufus. Unkind clerics claimed that this was a punishment for the King's dissolute life - but then the medieval church habitually slurred the memory of monarchs who had offended it. The modesty of the tower serves a purpose, for it does not distract the eye from the rest of the architecture and adornments, especially the magnificent west front.

The photographs that follow show the exterior of the Cathedral in all its splendour from the year 1886 to 1960. It has changed very little in the forty years since the last picture was taken, except for the opening of a worthy and informative visitor centre. The peace and tranquillity and the deep sense of history remain. A visit to Winchester should begin here, for this is the best place to grasp the importance, the power and the influence on king and priest on the rest of the city.

**FROM ST GILES 1886** 19401
The historic heart of old Winchester, once the capital of the Saxon kingdom of
Wessex, is seen here from the heights of St Giles hill. The great Norman Cathedral
dominates the scene as it has dominated Winchester's history.

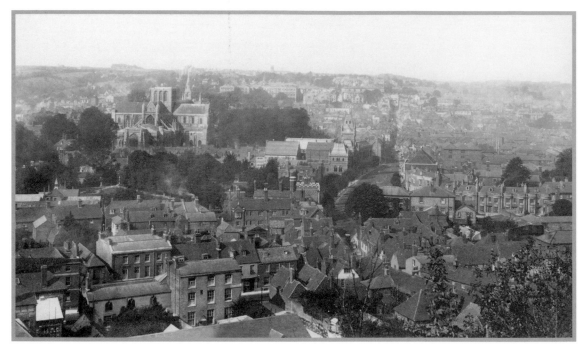

**GENERAL VIEW 1893** 32648

Winchester lies on the western banks of the River Itchen at a crossing important to Iron Age dwellers thousands of years ago. This was Alfred the Great's capital, and a favoured residence of many English kings and queens.

**FROM ST GILES HILL 1893** 32650

After the Roman invasion of AD43, old Iron Age enclosures were adapted to create the important Roman town of Venta Belgarum. Winchester remained an important settlement until the Romans withdrew in about 410. Much of the street pattern we see here is medieval in origin.

**FROM ST CATHERINE'S HILL 1899** 43675

Beyond the water meadows of the River Itchen is the Iron Age hillfort of St Catherine's Hill, the site of a maze which perhaps was used by penitent local monks, who would be blindfolded as they attempted to trace its paths. The view from the hill is one of the finest in Hampshire.

**FROM ST GILES HILL 1929** 81610

Looking along Broadway with the statue of Alfred the Great clearly visible, this view shows Winchester Cathedral in all its glory. Notice the army barracks on the hill beyond.

**THE CATHEDRAL 1886** 19407
A walk from the Square brings the
visitor across a green and open space
to the Norman Cathedral. Tourists
come from all over the world to visit
this architectural and spiritual gem.

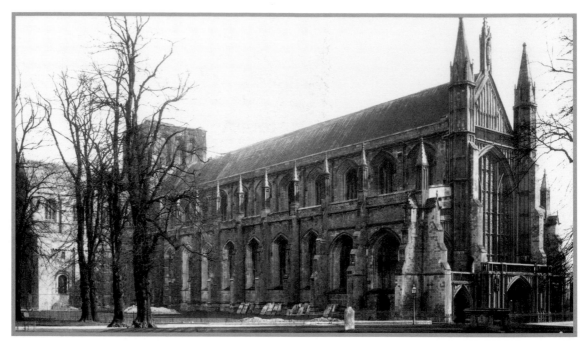

THE CATHEDRAL 1886 19406

THE CATHEDRAL 1886 19404

**THE CATHEDRAL 1886**
Christianity may have originally come to Winchester during the Roman occupation, though evidence suggests that the town did not become a religious centre until Saxon times. Many of the kings of Wessex were buried in the Saxon Cathedral, the foundations of which can be seen on this side of the present building.

**THE CATHEDRAL 1886**
The magnificent west front of Winchester Cathedral is seen here from its former burial ground. The beautifully-decorated Winchester Bible can be seen in the Cathedral Library. This 12th-century volume was hand-written by a single scribe over three years. The sumptuous decorations were prepared by several fine artists over a much longer period of time.

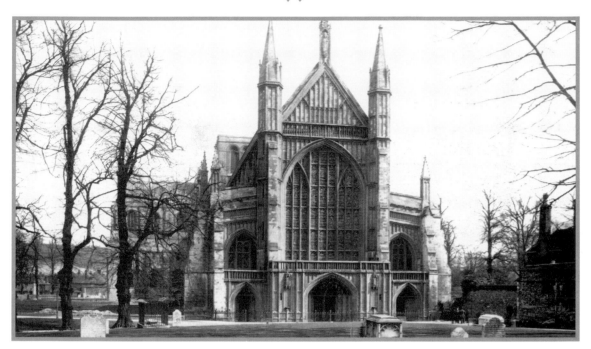

THE CATHEDRAL 1886   19403

THE CATHEDRAL 1886

Pilgrims came from all over the world to
pay homage at the Shrine of St Swithun,
a former Winchester Bishop. When the
Saint's body was moved from the
original burial place and into the
Norman Cathedral, a violent storm
broke out - perhaps the origin of St
Swithun's influence over the
British weather.

THE CATHEDRAL
*West Front 1909*
Buried in the Cathedral is Izaak Walton,
author of 'The Compleat Angler', who
died at his son-in-law's house in the
Cathedral Close in 1683. A
commemorative window was placed near
to his tomb as a gift from the fishermen
of England and America.

THE CATHEDRAL, WEST FRONT 1909   62178

**THE CATHEDRAL 1911** 63722
A splendid view of Winchester Cathedral. The original
Norman tower collapsed in 1107, some said because
King William Rufus - a monarch not popular with the
Church, though not really as bad as history has
painted him - had been buried underneath it after
being assassinated whilst hunting in the New Forest
seven years earlier.

**QUEEN MARY'S CHAIR 1911** 63730

**QUEEN MARY'S CHAIR 1911**
Queen Mary I, 'Bloody Mary', married Philip of Spain in Winchester Cathedral during Stephen Gardiner's time as Bishop. This marriage was to lead to conflict between England and Spain during the subsequent reign of Mary's sister Elizabeth.

◆

**THE CATHEDRAL 1922**
Jane Austen, the novelist, lies under a slab of marble in the north aisle of the Cathedral. She died at a house in College Street in 1817. Her tombstone shows no evidence of her being a writer - perhaps because it was considered to be an unsuitable employment for a woman at that time.

**THE CATHEDRAL 1922** 72488

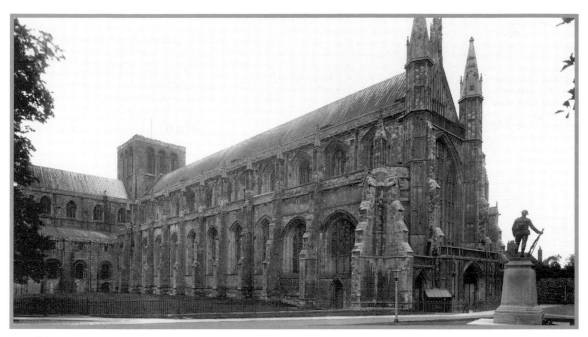

THE CATHEDRAL 1922  72487
Winchester Cathedral was built on marshy ground, and by 1905 serious subsidence had occurred. A deep-sea diver, William Walker, was employed to go deep into the marshy water beneath and shore up the building. A bronze statuette commemorates the brave man who saved Winchester Cathedral.

THE CATHEDRAL c1960  W107076
Winchester Cathedral is not just an historical monument, but a living place of worship. Services of Holy Communion, Matins and Evensong are held in the Cathedral every day.

**ST CROSS VILLAGE 1919** 68959

A stroll across the water meadows of the River Itchen brings the traveller to the village of St Cross, seen here just after the end of the First World War. One imagines that the small boy would have had some difficulty riding that particular bicycle.

**ST CROSS VILLAGE 1928** 80901

One visitor to St Cross was the poet John Keats, who stayed in Winchester during 1819 and often walked this way. It is said that his famous poem 'Ode to Autumn', which begins with the line 'Season of mists and mellow fruitfulness...', was written after one such ramble.

**ST CROSS 1896**  37/250

The Hospital of St Cross was founded by Bishop Henry de Blois, half-brother to King Stephen, in 1136. It is one of the oldest charitable establishments in England. Guided tours are available for those who visit this ancient site.

**ST CROSS CHURCH 1906**  55879

The Church at St Cross was begun in the 1130s and serves as both the parish church and the Hospital's chapel. It too was founded by Henry de Blois, and is an excellent example of the development from Norman to Early English architecture.

**ST CROSS HOSPITAL 1906** 55884
This house of charity was founded to provide for the daily feeding of 100 poor men and the housing and clothing of 13 more who could no longer look after themselves. The Hospital is still home to some 25 Brothers, who now live in apartments within the original complex.

**ST CROSS 1909** 61609
A second charitable foundation was made by Bishop Cardinal Beaufort in 1446: an Almshouse of Noble Poverty, for once-wealthy people who had fallen on hard times. Both foundations are represented at St Cross today, each with a different uniform - one red and one black.

**THE CHURCH OF ST CROSS 1919** 68960
A great deal of money was spent on the buildings of this charitable foundation. The roof of the Great Hall uses Spanish chestnut, while there is a great deal of ornate wooden panelling and early stained glass.

**THE CHURCH OF ST CROSS 1919** 68966
'Tickets for Sale' reads the sign to the left of the archway, as a member of the Brethren greets a visitor over eighty years ago. The tourist of today receives just as warm a welcome.

**ST CROSS 1919** 68967
Almshouses from the 15th century line the pleasant grounds of the Hospital of St Cross. It is hard to imagine a nicer or more peaceful place to spend one's old age.

**ST CROSS HOSPITAL, THE BRETHREN 1928** 80908
Every now and again, the Brothers gather in the mid 14th-century Brethren's Hall for a feast of celebration called the Gaudy Lunch.

**ST CROSS HOSPITAL**
*The Wayfarers Dole 1928*
By the rules of the foundation, for eight centuries travellers have been given bread and ale on demand - the Wayfarers Dole. If you visit St Cross Hospital and ask - even today - you will be given a portion of bread and a beaker of ale. A delightful custom. May it long continue!

**THE CHURCH OF ST CROSS c1960**
A visit to St Cross breaks down the barrier between past and present; it is a chance to glimpse the charitable values of medieval England - and to pause for a while from the hurry and bustle of the 21st century.

**ST CROSS HOSPITAL, THE WAYFARERS DOLE 1928** 80909

**THE CHURCH OF ST CROSS c1960** W107177

# City Streets and Landmarks

A GOOD PLACE to start an exploration of Winchester's streets is at the Buttercross, the 14th-century decorated monument that is everyone's favourite meeting place in the old city. How fortunate it was that the landowner who wished to remove the cross and use it as a garden ornament was thwarted by the loud protests of local people. Near here stood the Royal Palace of William the Conqueror. In the narrow passage leading from the Buttercross to the Square can be seen a column of stone; this is probably the last remaining portion of William's Winchester residence.

The Square itself is rich in history Originally part of what would have been the large cemetery of the nearby Cathedral, the Square became a venue for markets in the Middle Ages. It was also a place of execution, and the tolling of the bell of the Church of St Lawrence was the last sound to be heard by the unfortunates as their sentence was carried out. A plaque commemorates the execution of Lady Alice Lisle, who was brutally done to death here in 1685 for sheltering two rebels after the Duke of Monmouth's rebellion. Today the Square is a happier place of shops, restaurants and public houses, and benches to help take the weight off your feet as you tour Winchester.

The city mostly retains its medieval street pattern. A glance at the map produced by the cartographer John Speed in 1611 shows a town layout not very different to the one we know today. Certainly, by the end of the 12th century Winchester was second only to London in size, and it retained much of its old importance.

During the Anarchy, as the 'nineteen long winters' of King Stephen's reign is known, the city literally became a battleground between the King's half-brother Bishop Henry de Blois and Stephen's bitter enemy, the Empress Matilda. Winchester Castle was badly damaged and the old Norman Royal Palace was destroyed, and much of the town was burnt and razed to the ground during the siege and attack of 1141. Winchester took some years to recover.

Broadway and the High Street, which lead up from the River Itchen, may be sited along the route of an ancient trackway. The High Street of today ends at Westgate, one of two surviving medieval city gates in Winchester and a very prominent landmark. Its narrow archway had to cope with the demands of modern traffic until well into the 20th century. It is not only an excellent example of a fortification of its period, but contains also an informative museum and provides a viewpoint over much of the central part of the city.

There are several other lovely old buildings pictured in this section of the book. But they are just a sample of the joys of Winchester's building legacy, giving us a feeling that the Frith photographers were somewhat spoiled for choice. From the Tudor magnificence of God Begot House, to the gothic Victorian of the New Guildhall, Winchester is a dream come true for both the historian and the student of architecture.

But buildings and history alone do not make a city. In these photographs are the people of Winchester's more recent history - residents and tourists alike. Study the fashions of the day, and note the behaviour of the passers-by, from respectably-clad Victorians gossiping on a street corner to tiny boys posing for the camera, from the bicyclist to the driver of early motor cars, from policemen on watchful duty to window shoppers. These people are all a reminder that human nature, like the stones of old Winchester, never really changes.

HIGH STREET FROM WESTGATE 1906  55859

**CITY CROSS 1886** 19443
The Buttercross is everyone's meeting place in Winchester; in the next few photographs we can see how the townscape around it changed over some seventy years. Notice in particular the transformation of the shops and businesses in the background.

**CITY CROSS 1893** 32655

Buttercross dates from the 15th century. It almost disappeared in the 1700s, when it just escaped being sold to an influential local landowner as a garden ornament. Thanks to the angry protests of local people it remained in its original position.

**BUTTERCROSS 1899** 43677

By the end of the 19th century the building behind the cross had abandoned its role as a general store and had become a refreshment house. This must have been in recognition of Winchester's growing role as a tourist centre.

**HIGH STREET 1906** 55856
As the 'Tea' sign indicates, refreshments for passers-by
were a part of Edwardian life in Winchester. But the
main shop had become that most delightful of
institutions - a traditional sweet shop.

**HIGH STREET 1928** 80882

By the 1920s motor cars had largely replaced the horses and carts seen in the earlier photographs. It is interesting to note how, in the interests of fashion, everyone is wearing a hat. Can you spot the watchful city policeman?

**HIGH STREET c1955** W107066

Allen's Confectioners remained on the site when this photograph was taken in the 1950s. In the closing years of the 20th century, motor traffic became such a problem in the narrow roads of the old city that High Street was pedestrianised.

**THE PENTICE 1928** 80888

The covered walkway of The Pentice was created when the upper floor of its houses was extended in the 16th century. Until 1279 a Royal Mint of the Norman and Angevin kings stood on the site.

**THE PENTICE c1955** W107040

By the 1950s the habitual wearing of hats and caps might have become a fashion of the past, but strolling through the old streets of Winchester was increasing in popularity, as we can see from the large number of pedestrians.

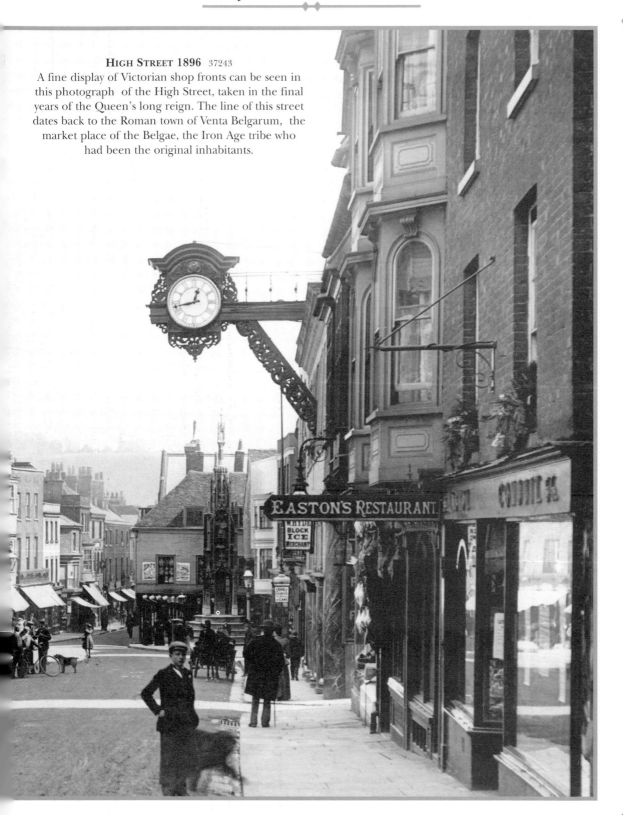

**HIGH STREET 1896** 37243
A fine display of Victorian shop fronts can be seen in this photograph of the High Street, taken in the final years of the Queen's long reign. The line of this street dates back to the Roman town of Venta Belgarum, the market place of the Belgae, the Iron Age tribe who had been the original inhabitants.

EASTON'S RESTAURANT

**HIGH STREET 1899** 43685
The town clock, which has a statue
of Queen Anne in a niche behind,
was presented to the city after a
royal visit in 1713. The building
behind is the old Guildhall.

**HIGH STREET 1906** 55858

**HIGH STREET FROM WESTGATE 1906** 55859

**HIGH STREET 1906**
Edwardians take a stroll along the upper end of High Street, with the old fortification of Westgate in view. Almost every monarch since William the Conqueror has passed this way

◆

**HIGH STREET FROM WESTGATE 1906**
This view looks back along the High Street from the top of Westgate's defensive tower. From any high point in the city it is quite easy to identify parts of the medieval street layout.

**WESTGATE 1896** 37245

Westgate is one of the most prominent landmarks in Winchester. In the following pictures we see how it retains its importance as an historic and architectural feature as the city changes around it. Notice the old city wall pub, the Plume of Feathers, to the right of the gate.

**WESTGATE 1909** 62175

Westgate dominated the western defences of the old city. It dates originally from the 12th century, and was reinforced during the Hundred Years War in anticipation of an attack by the French. The entire structure stands on the site of an earlier Roman fortification.

**WESTGATE AND HIGH STREET 1911**  63747
This view through Westgate's archway would have been glimpsed by generations of early travellers. Properly garrisoned medieval cities could sustain lengthy sieges by marauding armies.

### WESTGATE 1906

Westgate has many of the hallmarks of a medieval defensive work, including 'murder holes' from which heavy weights or boiling oils and molten lead might be dropped during an attack, while the slits below the shields were used for firing early guns. A portcullis would have dropped down to close off the archway.

### WESTGATE MUSEUM 1911

For well over a century the room above Westgate's arch has functioned as a small museum. It still houses the excellent collection of historic weights and measures and the instruments of torture shown here.

**WESTGATE 1906**  55860

**WESTGATE MUSEUM 1911**  63748

**FROM WESTGATE 1923** 74230

Traffic climbs the hill from High Street towards Westgate. The kinds of traffic may change, but the importance of Westgate as a city monument remains. There must always have been excellent views towards Winchester Cathedral.

**WESTGATE c1955**  W107057

By the 1950s the Plume of Feathers was no more, and its site was derelict. As the warning notices indicate, 20th-century traffic was having difficulty coping with the narrow but historic arch.

**WESTGATE c1960**  W107105

This was the solution to the traffic problem. After several hundred years as the main western entrance to the town, Westgate was bypassed - the old Plume of Feathers became just a distant memory.

**HIGH STREET 1909** 62172
Not far from this part of the High Street is Staple
Gardens, a street that predates even the Norman
Conquest; it is Saxon in origin, dating to that glorious
period when Winchester was the capital of Alfred's
Kingdom of Wessex. An important wool market was
held at Staple Gardens in the Middle Ages.

**HIGH STREET 1909** 62171

A walk down High Street from Westgate to the Buttercross takes the sightseer along one of the most ancient streets in the realm. On the right-hand side of the road, halfway down, is the old Guildhall, where the city's curfew bell is rung at 8pm each evening.

**HIGH STREET 1928**  80885

Here we see policemen on point duty in the 1920s, coping with an increasing amount of traffic
that began to bedevil Winchester's streets during the last century -
a reminder that medieval streets were never designed with the motor car in mind.

**HIGH STREET 1928**  80887

HIGH STREET 1928  80886

**HIGH STREET c1955** W107026

A quarter of a century apart, this and the previous view of the High Street show how little it changed throughout the 20th century, with the exception of traffic problems and an increased number of tourists. Apart from the introduction of a pedestrianisation scheme and some new shop fronts, it remains much the same today.

**THE SQUARE 1909** 62174

Just across from Winchester Cathedral is The Square. In the background is the Norman church of St Lawrence, which tradition suggests was the chapel of William the Conqueror's royal palace. New Bishops of Winchester traditionally pray here before being enthroned.

**THE SQUARE 1936** 87173
Public executions were held in The Square in earlier days, with the bell of St Lawrence's tolling mournfully as the victim was brought before the crowd. The Square of today is a happier place, popular with those tourists who want a good view of the Cathedral.

**ST GILES HILL 1899** 42968
St Giles Hill is the high ground to the east of the old city walls. A fine view over the city can be had by crossing the River Itchen and ascending to its summit. A famous fair used to be held on the hillside.

**STATION HILL 1909** 61602
The coming of the railway brought new prosperity to
cities such as Winchester, encouraging tourism and
new industries. The success of the Permanent Way led
to a decline in the use of the old stagecoach routes - a
decline not reversed until the heyday of the motor car.

**THE OLDEST HOUSE (OLD CHESIL RECTORY) 1896** 37247

This late medieval building in Chesil Street is one of Winchester's oldest surviving buildings, dating from around 1450. It has served the city as a popular restaurant for many years.

**THE OLD CHESIL RECTORY c1955** W107020

**KING ALFRED'S STATUE 1899**  43677A
This dramatic statue of Alfred the Great, King of Wessex, occupies a prominent site in Broadway. The bronze statue was fashioned by the sculptor Hamo Thornycroft to mark the 1000th anniversary of Alfred's rule.

**BROADWAY AND KING ALFRED'S STATUE 1909** 61600
Broadway and its continuation, the High Street, almost
certainly follow the line of an ancient trackway that
crossed the River Itchen during the Iron Age. It has
remained the principal eastern approach to Winchester.

**CITY BRIDGE 1906** 55867

Legend relates that the original city bridge was built by St Swithun, the former Bishop and patron saint of Winchester. The present bridge dates back to 1813.

**WESTGATE AND NEW BUILDINGS 1896** 37246

Victorian architects designed these buildings to be in considerable sympathy with the traditional buildings of Winchester. At the time that this photograph was taken, the corner building was the headquarters of the Hampshire Friendly Society.

**THE ROUND TABLE 1906**
The Round Table of King Arthur, made supposedly by the magician Merlin, has hung in Winchester's Great Hall for some six hundred years. In fact, it was probably made in the 13th century and restored in Tudor times, when the face of a young Henry VIII was added to the portrait of the legendary Arthur.

**THE ROUND TABLE 1906** 55874

**THE ROUND TABLE 1906** 55873

**THE GREAT HALL 1912** 64458

**KINGSGATE 1911** 63734

### THE GREAT HALL 1912
The present Great Hall of Winchester Castle was rebuilt during the reign of Henry III. When the castle was demolished, the hall was kept as a courtroom; it was here that Sir Walter Raleigh was sentenced to death in 1603.

### KINGSGATE 1911
Kingsgate, surmounted by the little church of St Swithun-upon-Kingsgate, is one of just two surviving medieval gateways at Winchester. Just around the corner from here is the house where the novelist Jane Austen died.

**GOD BEGOT HOUSE 1909** 62177

**YE OLDE HOSTEL OF GOD BEGOT 1929**
The present God Begot House is Tudor, though it stands on the site of an ancient manor originally bequeathed by Emma, widow of King Canute, to the Priory of St Swithun in 1052. Lawbreakers could seek sanctuary at God Begot House during the Middle Ages.

◆

**ABBEY GARDENS 1923**
The Abbey Gardens are a popular city park, overshadowed now by the new Guildhall. Abbey House is the official residence of the Mayor of Winchester. The area was the site of St Mary's Abbey, founded by Alfred the Great's Queen.

**YE OLDE HOSTEL OF GOD BEGOT 1929**  81625

**ABBEY GARDENS 1923**  74232

**THE HOSPITAL 1906** 55876

As an important cathedral city, Winchester established an important tradition of tending the sick,
probably from the days when pilgrims came to the shrine of St Swithun in search of miraculous cures.
We see here fine examples of Victorian architecture.

**R.H.C. HOSPITAL 1909** 61604

ST JOHN'S ALMSHOUSE 1911  63740

The gardens of many of these erstwhile charitable foundations are havens of peace and tranquillity,
away from the bustle of the city. Some visitors still emulate the old tradition
of making a personal pilgrimage to the city of Winchester.

CHRIST'S HOSPITAL 1911  63742

THE GUILDHALL **1886** 19423

A monument to Victorian self-confidence, the Guildhall is built in the popular Gothic revival style and was opened in 1873. Today it is a favourite venue for artistic events and conferences.

THE GUILDHALL **1936** 87172

Near to the site of the Guildhall once stood the Nunnaminster, one of the three royal monasteries of Saxon Winchester, founded in about 903 by Ealhswith, the widow of Alfred the Great.

# Round and About

TRAVELLERS OF ALL kinds have passed through the countryside around Winchester for a variety of reasons, from Iron Age warriors to Roman legionnaires, medieval pilgrims, sailors and merchants to the tourists of today. Many still find their way to the ancient capital of Wessex, and for just as many reasons: some deliberately to view the beautiful Cathedral and other historic buildings in the city, others to buy goods from an impressive array of modern shops, or maybe just to explore the countryside and the towns and villages thereabouts.

Winchester College is the oldest public school in England, founded by William of Wykeham in 1382, with a dedication to the Virgin Mary. 'Manners Makyth Man' runs the school motto, and time spent in Winchester probably does much good in shaping the characters of the pupils - or Wykehamists, as they are called. Perhaps it gives them all an abiding interest in the history and architecture of the Middle Ages, if nothing else. Scholars in olden times led a Spartan existence; electricity was only introduced in 1930, and for another thirty years the boys had to bathe in tin baths filled with cold water.

Guided walks take the interested visitor around several of the college buildings, which have been used since its foundation and are still in use today. There might be a chance, if the timing is right, to hear the singing of the college choir, supplemented by the younger quiristers from the Pilgrims School - the Cathedral's choir school - echoing out of the 14th-century college chapel.

A ramble across the water meadows of the Itchen to the downlands above will show the walker just how old this landscape is. On St Catherine's Hill is a famous Iron Age hillfort, while further out are Bronze Age barrows, Roman roads and villa sites.

Thanks to their proximity to Winchester and the larger city of Southampton, many of the towns and villages grew considerably in size during the 20th century, but all are worthy of exploration. A pretty walk - if the modern roads can be avoided - is the journey to the Worthies. Both Headbourne Worthy and Kings Worthy have been developed since these photographs were taken, but they are well worth a visit. Headbourne Worthy has an excellent Saxon church, much of it older than the neighbouring Winchester Cathedral. Tradition alleges that the Saxon Wilfrid built the first place of worship here on this site, though some of the building might date from the reign of Edward the Confessor. After the Reformation Henry VIII gave the Worthies to his one beloved queen, Jane Seymour.

A longer walk to the south of Winchester brings the visitor to Twyford, situated like its larger neighbour on a particularly old crossing point over the River Itchen. The 'Queen of Hampshire Villages' was also increased in size and population since these photographs were taken, but as an historic a

Saxon settlement, and given its connections with the poet and satirist Alexander Pope, should be visited.

The River Itchen has helped shape the destinies of many of the communities along its banks; it should be followed from source to mouth, halting at each settlement along the journey - this would be a most interesting way to get a grasp of the social history of this part of England. From its prettiest water meadows and the heights of the downs come distant views of Winchester and its Cathedral - seen in the way that pilgrims of the past would have first regarded the 'city of kings and priests'.

**STREET SCENE 1906** 53493
Here we see an empty street on the approaches to Winchester during the long 'afternoon' of Edward VII's reign. Notice the absence of any traffic, apart from one solitary horse and cart - the streets around the city are a little more crowded a century later.

**WINCHESTER COLLEGE, RIDDING FIELD 1919** 68956

These are the playing fields of Winchester College. Winchester College was founded by William of Wykeham in 1387, and is the oldest public school in England. The college was originally founded to prepare 70 poor scholars for entry to New College, Oxford, and then for the priesthood.

**WINCHESTER COLLEGE 1922** 72493

Many of the original buildings of Winchester College remain, and are still used by today's pupils. The college chapel was originally consecrated around the year 1394. In the cloister nearby is the grave of Field Marshall Lord Wavell - one of a distinguished line of 'old boys'.

**WINCHESTER COLLEGE FROM THE CATHEDRAL 1929** 81611
Until the 1960s, Winchester's pupils led a Spartan existence, bathing every day in cold water in tin baths; perhaps this helped generations of schoolboys to face the rigours of life outside and to live up to the school motto: 'Manners Makyth Man'.

**STANMORE FROM ROMSEY ROAD 1928** 80896
Romsey Road leads westward away from the city centre and towards the rolling downlands of Hampshire. Winchester is an excellent touring centre for exploring one of the most ancient landscapes in Britain.

**THE BARRACKS c1960** W107111
Winchester has always been an important centre for military training; much of the countryside round and about is used for tactical exercises. The barracks, close to Westgate, contain several interesting military museums.

**HURSLEY, THE CHURCH 1886** 19446
In Hursley church, southwest of Winchester, lies the body of Richard Cromwell, the famous 'Tumbledown Dick' of history, who succeeded his father Oliver Cromwell as Lord Protector of England for a few months before the restoration of King Charles II.

**HEADBOURNE WORTHY, THE CHURCH AND THE LYCHGATE 1912** 64462
The church of Headbourne Worthy is one of the oldest in southern England: it stood for long years before William the Conqueror won the realm at the Battle of Hastings in 1066. In the churchyard lies the Stuart scholar Joseph Bingham, author of a famous work on Christian antiquities.

**KINGS WORTHY, THE CHURCH 1912** 64469
On the old highway leading north out of Winchester is Kings Worthy, a large village of considerable antiquity. The church has been sympathetically restored, though the flint tower is 15th-century.

**KINGS WORTHY, THE CHURCH AND THE LYCHGATE 1912** 64468
In the churchyard is the grave of the great Victorian Liberal Shaw Lefevre, Lord Eversley, who worked closely with the long-serving Prime Minister Mr Gladstone. Lefevre was a people's champion, for he defended public footpaths and common lands. He was born in the reign of William IV and died aged 97 during the reign of George V.

**KINGS WORTHY, THE VILLAGE 1912** 64467
In this village in the early years of the last century lived four brothers, Ernest, Cecil, Reginald and Charles Baring. All four lost their lives in the First World War. A plaque in the church marks their tragic passing.

**KINGS WORTHY, AVINGTON MANSION c1960** K143009
Above the banks of the River Itchen stands Avington Mansion. Many of the grand country houses, parks and estates of Hampshire are now popular attractions, within easy travelling distance of Winchester.

**TWYFORD, THE 1000-YEAR-OLD YEW TREE c1955** T284004
An ancient yew tree shows the antiquity of many a country churchyard. Yew was used in the manufacture of the traditional English longbow, which turned the tide of battle at Crecy and Agincourt.

**TWYFORD, HIGH STREET c1955** T284010
The 'Queen of Hampshire Villages', Twyford, now a very large settlement, belonged to the See of Winchester from Saxon times. The poet Alexander Pope attended school here, and was expelled for lampooning his schoolmaster in verse.

**TWYFORD, QUEEN STREET c1965** T284014
One 18th-century resident of Twyford was Mrs Maria Fitzherbert, who spent much of her childhood here, before going to London and becoming the mistress of the Prince of Wales - later George IV. Local tradition alleges that she married Prince George in secret at nearby Brambridge House.

**TWYFORD**
*The Church of England School c1965*
The local school is at the heart of many an English community, being used for many local occasions after the end of the school day.

**TWYFORD**
*Queen Street and the Volunteer Inn c1965*
Twyford, as the name suggests, stands on an ancient crossing place over the River Itchen. The downlands hereabouts bear the marks of Iron Age dwellers who occupied this valley three thousand years ago.

TWYFORD, THE CHURCH OF ENGLAND SCHOOL C1965   T284624

TWYFORD, QUEEN STREET AND THE VOLUNTEER INN C1965   T284026

**TWYFORD, THE CHURCH FROM THE RIVER ITCHEN c1965** T284032
The 140-ft tower and spire of Twyford Church dominate the banks of the nearby River Itchen. This is a pleasant place to sit on a summer's evening, and admire the ancient landscape that makes Winchester and Hampshire such a delightful place to visit.

# Index

# Frith Book Co Titles

Town Books 96pp, 100 photos. County and Themed Books 128pp, 150 photos (unless specified) All titles hardback laminated case and jacket except those indicated pb (paperback)

| | | |
|---|---|---|
| Around Barnstaple | 1-85937-084-5 | £12.99 |
| Around Blackpool | 1-85937-049-7 | £12.99 |
| Around Bognor Regis | 1-85937-055-1 | £12.99 |
| Around Bristol | 1-85937-050-0 | £12.99 |
| Around Cambridge | 1-85937-092-6 | £12.99 |
| Cheshire | 1-85937-045-4 | £14.99 |
| Around Chester | 1-85937-090-X | £12.99 |
| Around Chesterfield | 1-85937-071-3 | £12.99 |
| Around Chichester | 1-85937-089-6 | £12.99 |
| Cornwall | 1-85937-054-3 | £14.99 |
| Cotswolds | 1-85937-099-3 | £14.99 |
| Around Derby | 1-85937-046-2 | £12.99 |
| Devon | 1-85937-052-7 | £14.99 |
| Dorset | 1-85937-075-6 | £14.99 |
| Dorset Coast | 1-85937-062-4 | £14.99 |
| Around Dublin | 1-85937-058-6 | £12.99 |
| East Anglia | 1-85937-059-4 | £14.99 |
| Around Eastbourne | 1-85937-061-6 | £12.99 |
| English Castles | 1-85937-078-0 | £14.99 |
| Around Falmouth | 1-85937-066-7 | £12.99 |
| Hampshire | 1-85937-064-0 | £14.99 |
| Isle of Man | 1-85937-065-9 | £14.99 |
| Around Maidstone | 1-85937-056-X | £12.99 |
| North Yorkshire | 1-85937-048-9 | £14.99 |
| Around Nottingham | 1-85937-060-8 | £12.99 |
| Around Penzance | 1-85937-069-1 | £12.99 |
| Around Reading | 1-85937-087-X | £12.99 |
| Around St Ives | 1-85937-068-3 | £12.99 |
| Around Salisbury | 1-85937-091-8 | £12.99 |
| Around Scarborough | 1-85937-104-3 | £12.99 |
| Scottish Castles | 1-85937-077-2 | £14.99 |
| Around Sevenoaks and Tonbridge | 1-85937-057-8 | £12.99 |

| | | |
|---|---|---|
| Sheffield and S Yorkshire | 1-85937-070-5 | £14.99 |
| Shropshire | 1-85937-083-7 | £14.99 |
| Staffordshire | 1-85937-047-0 (96pp) | £12.99 |
| Suffolk | 1-85937-074-8 | £14.99 |
| Surrey | 1-85937-081-0 | £14.99 |
| Around Torbay | 1-85937-063-2 | £12.99 |
| Wiltshire | 1-85937-053-5 | £14.99 |
| Around Bakewell | 1-85937-113-2 | £12.99 |
| Around Bournemouth | 1-85937-067-5 | £12.99 |
| Cambridgeshire | 1-85937-086-1 | £14.99 |
| Essex | 1-85937-082-9 | £14.99 |
| Around Great Yarmouth | 1-85937-085-3 | £12.99 |
| Hertfordshire | 1-85937-079-9 | £14.99 |
| Isle of Wight | 1-85937-114-0 | £14.99 |
| Around Lincoln | 1-85937-111-6 | £12.99 |
| Oxfordshire | 1-85937-076-4 | £14.99 |
| Around Shrewsbury | 1-85937-110-8 | £12.99 |
| South Devon Coast | 1-85937-107-8 | £14.99 |
| Around Stratford upon Avon | 1-85937-098-5 | £12.99 |
| West Midlands | 1-85937-109-4 | £14.99 |

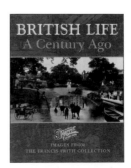

**British Life A Century Ago**
246 x 189mm
144pp, hardback.
Black and white
Lavishly illustrated with photos from the turn of the century, and with extensive commentary. It offers a unique insight into the social history and heritage of bygone Britain.

1-85937-103-5  £17.99

# Available from your local bookshop or from the publisher

# Frith Book Co Titles Available in 2000

| | | | |
|---|---|---|---|
| Around Bath | 1-85937-097-7 | £12.99 | Mar |
| County Durham | 1-85937-123-x | £14.99 | Mar |
| Cumbria | 1-85937-101-9 | £14.99 | Mar |
| Down the Thames | 1-85937-121-3 | £14.99 | Mar |
| Around Exeter | 1-85937-126-4 | £12.99 | Mar |
| Greater Manchester | 1-85937-108-6 | £14.99 | Mar |
| Around Guildford | 1-85937-117-5 | £12.99 | Mar |
| Around Harrogate | 1-85937-112-4 | £12.99 | Mar |
| Around Leicester | 1-85937-073-x | £12.99 | Mar |
| Around Liverpool | 1-85937-051-9 | £12.99 | Mar |
| Around Newark | 1-85937-105-1 | £12.99 | Mar |
| Northumberland and Tyne & Wear | | | |
| | 1-85937-072-1 | £14.99 | Mar |
| Around Oxford | 1-85937-096-9 | £12.99 | Mar |
| Around Plymouth | 1-85937-119-1 | £12.99 | Mar |
| Around Southport | 1-85937-106-x | £12.99 | Mar |
| Welsh Castles | 1-85937-120-5 | £14.99 | Mar |
| | | | |
| Around Belfast | 1-85937-094-2 | £12.99 | Apr |
| Canals and Waterways | 1-85937-129-9 | £17.99 | Apr |
| Down the Severn | 1-85937-118-3 | £14.99 | Apr |
| East Sussex | 1-85937-130-2 | £14.99 | Apr |
| Exmoor | 1-85937-132-9 | £14.99 | Apr |
| Gloucestershire | 1-85937-102-7 | £14.99 | Apr |
| Around Horsham | 1-85937-127-2 | £12.99 | Apr |
| Around Ipswich | 1-85937-133-7 | £12.99 | Apr |
| Ireland (pb) | 1-85937-181-7 | £9.99 | Apr |
| Kent Living Memories | 1-85937-125-6 | £14.99 | Apr |
| London (pb) | 1-85937-183-3 | £9.99 | Apr |
| New Forest | 1-85937-128-0 | £14.99 | Apr |
| Scotland (pb) | 1-85937-182-5 | £9.99 | Apr |
| Around Southampton | 1-85937-088-8 | £12.99 | Apr |
| Stone Circles & Ancient Monuments | | | |
| | 1-85937-143-4 | £17.99 | Apr |
| Sussex (pb) | 1-85937-184-1 | £9.99 | Apr |
| | | | |
| Colchester (pb) | 1-85937-188-4 | £8.99 | May |
| County Maps of Britain | | | |
| | 1-85937-156-6 (192pp) | £19.99 | May |
| Leicestershire (pb) | 1-85937-185-x | £9.99 | May |
| Lincolnshire | 1-85937-135-3 | £14.99 | May |
| Around Newquay | 1-85937-140-x | £12.99 | May |
| Nottinghamshire (pb) | 1-85937-187-6 | £9.99 | May |
| Redhill to Reigate | 1-85937-137-x | £12.99 | May |
| Victorian & Edwardian Yorkshire | | | |
| | 1-85937-154-x | £14.99 | May |
| Around Winchester | 1-85937-139-6 | £12.99 | May |
| Yorkshire (pb) | 1-85937-186-8 | £9.99 | May |
| | | | |
| Berkshire (pb) | 1-85937-191-4 | £9.99 | Jun |
| Brighton (pb) | 1-85937-192-2 | £8.99 | Jun |
| Dartmoor | 1-85937-145-0 | £14.99 | Jun |
| East London | 1-85937-080-2 | £14.99 | Jun |
| Glasgow (pb) | 1-85937-190-6 | £8.99 | Jun |
| Kent (pb) | 1-85937-189-2 | £9.99 | Jun |
| Victorian & Edwardian Kent | | | |
| | 1-85937-149-3 | £14.99 | Jun |
| North Devon Coast | 1-85937-146-9 | £14.99 | Jun |
| Peak District | 1-85937-100-0 | £14.99 | Jun |
| Around Truro | 1-85937-147-7 | £12.99 | Jun |
| Victorian & Edwardian Maritime Album | | | |
| | 1-85937-144-2 | £17.99 | Jun |
| West Sussex | 1-85937-148-5 | £14.99 | Jun |
| | | | |
| Churches of Berkshire | 1-85937-170-1 | £17.99 | Jul |
| Churches of Dorset | 1-85937-172-8 | £17.99 | Jul |
| Churches of Hampshire | 1-85937-207-4 | £17.99 | Jul |
| Churches of Wiltshire | 1-85937-171-x | £17.99 | Jul |
| Derbyshire (pb) | 1-85937-196-5 | £9.99 | Jul |
| Edinburgh (pb) | 1-85937-193-0 | £8.99 | Jul |
| Herefordshire | 1-85937-174-4 | £14.99 | Jul |
| Norwich (pb) | 1-85937-194-9 | £8.99 | Jul |
| Ports and Harbours | 1-85937-208-2 | £17.99 | Jul |
| Somerset and Avon | 1-85937-153-1 | £14.99 | Jul |
| South Devon Living Memories | | | |
| | 1-85937-168-x | £14.99 | Jul |
| Warwickshire (pb) | 1-85937-203-1 | £9.99 | Jul |
| Worcestershire | 1-85937-152-3 | £14.99 | Jul |
| Yorkshire Living Memories | | | |
| | 1-85937-166-3 | £14.99 | Jul |

# FRITH PRODUCTS & SERVICES

Francis Frith would doubtless be pleased to know that the pioneering publishing venture he started in 1860 still continues today. More than a hundred and thirty years later, The Francis Frith Collection continues in the same innovative tradition and is now one of the foremost publishers of vintage photographs in the world. Some of the current activities include:

## Interior Decoration

Today Frith's photographs can be seen framed and as giant wall murals in thousands of pubs, restaurants, hotels, banks, retail stores and other public buildings throughout the country. In every case they enhance the unique local atmosphere of the places they depict and provide reminders of gentler days in an increasingly busy and frenetic world.

## Product Promotions

Frith products have been used by many major companies to promote the sales of their own products or to reinforce their own history and heritage. Brands include Hovis bread, Courage beers, Scots Porage Oats, Colman's mustard, Cadbury's foods, Mellow Birds coffee, Dunhill pipe tobacco, Guinness, and Bulmer's Cider.

## Genealogy and Family History

As the interest in family history and roots grows world-wide, more and more people are turning to Frith's photographs of Great Britain for images of the towns, villages and streets where their ancestors lived; and, of course, photographs of the churches and chapels where their ancestors were christened, married and buried are an essential part of every genealogy tree and family album.

A series of easy-to-use CD Roms is planned for publication, and an increasing number of Frith photographs will be able to be viewed on specialist genealogy sites. A growing range of Frith books will be available on CD.

## The Internet

Already thousands of Frith photographs can be viewed and purchased on the internet. By the end of the year 2000 some 60,000 Frith photographs will be available on the internet. The number of sites is constantly expanding, each focussing on different products and services from the Collection.

Some of the sites are listed below.

www.townpages.co.uk
www.icollector.com
www.barclaysquare.co.uk
www.cornwall-online.co.uk

For background information on the Collection look at the three following sites:

www.francisfrith.com
www.francisfrith.co.uk
www.frithbook.co.uk

## Frith Products

All Frith photographs are available Framed or just as Mounted Prints, and can be ordered from the address below. From time to time other products - Address Books, Calendars, Table Mats, etc - are available.

> **For further information:**
> if you would like further information on any of the above aspects of the Frith business please contact us at the address below:
> **The Francis Frith Collection,**
> **Frith's Barn, Teffont, Salisbury, Wiltshire,**
> **England SP3 5QP.**
> Tel: +44 (0)1722 716 376  Fax: +44 (0)1722 716 881  Email: uksales@francisfrith.com

# To receive your FREE Mounted Print

**Mounted Print**
*Overall size 14 x 11 inches*

*Cut out this Voucher and return it with your remittance for £1.50 to cover postage and handling. Choose any photograph included in this book. Your SEPIA print will be A4 in size, and mounted in a cream mount with burgundy rule lines, overall size 14 x 11 inches.*

## Order additional Mounted Prints at HALF PRICE (only £7.49 each*)

If there are further pictures you would like to order, possibly as gifts for friends and family, acquire them at half price (no additional postage and handling required).

## Have your Mounted Prints framed*

For an additional £14.95 per print you can have your chosen Mounted Print framed in an elegant polished wood and gilt moulding, overall size 16 x 13 inches (no additional postage and handling required).

---

**\* IMPORTANT!**
**These special prices are only available if ordered using the original voucher on this page (no copies permitted) and at the same time as your free Mounted Print, for delivery to the same address**

---

## Frith Collectors' Guild

*From time to time we publish a magazine of news and stories about Frith photographs and further special offers of Frith products. If you would like 12 months FREE membership, please return this form.*

*Send completed forms to:*
**The Francis Frith Collection, Frith's Barn, Teffont, Salisbury, Wiltshire SP3 5QP**

---

 **for FREE and Reduced Price Frith Prints**

| Picture no. | Page number | Qty | Mounted @ £7.49 | Framed + £14.95 | Total Cost |
|---|---|---|---|---|---|
| | | 1 | **Free of charge*** | £ | £ |
| | | | £7.49 | £ | £ |
| | | | £7.49 | £ | £ |
| | | | £7.49 | £ | £ |
| | | | £7.49 | £ | £ |
| | | | £7.49 | £ | £ |
| | | | \* Post & handling | | £1.50 |
| **Book Title** . . . . . . . . . . . . . . . | | | **Total Order Cost** | | £ |

***Please do not photocopy this voucher. Only the original is valid, so please cut it out and return it to us.***

I enclose a cheque / postal order for £ . . . . . . . . . .
made payable to 'The Francis Frith Collection'
OR please debit my Mastercard / Visa / Switch / Amex card

Number . . . . . . . . . . . . . . . . . . . . . . . . . . . . . . .

Expires . . . . . . . . . . . Signature . . . . . . . . . . . . . . . . . . . . . . .

Name Mr/Mrs/Ms . . . . . . . . . . . . . . . . . . . . . . . . . . . . . . . . . . . . .

Address . . . . . . . . . . . . . . . . . . . . . . . . . . . . . . . . . . . . . . . . . . .

. . . . . . . . . . . . . . . . . . . . . . . . . . . . . . . . . . . . . . . . . . . . . . . . . .

. . . . . . . . . . . . . . . . . . . . . . . . . . . . . . . . . . . . . . . . . . . . . . . . . .

. . . . . . . . . . . . . . . . . . . . . . . . . . . . . . . . . . . . . . . . . . . . . . . . . .

. . . . . . . . . . . . . . . . . . . . . . . . . Postcode . . . . . . . . . . . . . . . . . .

Daytime Tel No . . . . . . . . . . . . . . . . . . . . . . . . .          Valid to 31/12/01

---

## The Francis Frith Collectors' Guild

Please enrol me as a member for 12 months free of charge.

Name Mr/Mrs/Ms . . . . . . . . . . . . . . . . . . . . . . . . . . . . . . . . . . . . . . . . . .

Address . . . . . . . . . . . . . . . . . . . . . . . . . . . . . . . . . . . . . . . . . . . . . . . . .

. . . . . . . . . . . . . . . . . . . . . . . . . . . . . . . . . . . . . . . . . . . . . . . . . . . . . . .

. . . . . . . . . . . . . . . . . . . . . . . . . Postcode . . . . . . . . . . . . . . . . . . . . . . . .

Free Print - see overleaf